BE THOU MY SONG

Grace & Faith in Christian Poetry of the 17ᵗʰ Century

Grace & Faith in
Christian Poetry of
the 17th Century

BE
THOU
MY
SONG

KERRI L. TOM

Foreword by
STEVEN P. MUELLER

FIFTEEN-SEVENTEEN PUBLISHING
1517

Published by:
1517 Publishing
PO Box 54032
Irvine, CA 92619-4032

Publisher's Cataloging-In-Publication Data
(Prepared by The Donohue Group, Inc.)

Names: Tom, Kerri L., author. | Mueller, Steven P., 1964- writer of foreword.
Title: Be thou my song : grace and faith in Christian poetry of the seventeenth
    century / Kerri L. Tom ; foreword by Steven P. Mueller.
Description: Irvine, CA : 1517 Publishing, [2024] | Includes bibliographical
    references.
Identifiers: ISBN: 978-1-956658-89-7 (paperback) | 978-1-956658-75-0 (ebook)
Subjects: LCSH: Christian poetry, English—17th century. | Christian poetry,
    English—17th century— History and criticism. | Lutheran Church. | Grace
    (Theology)—Poetry. | Faith—Poetry. | Bible— Evidences, authority,
    etc.—Poetry. | BISAC: POETRY / Subjects & Themes / Inspirational &
    Religious. | POETRY / Subjects & Themes / General. | RELIGION /
    Christian Living / General.
Classification: LCC: PR1195.C48 T66 2024 | DDC: 821.00803823—dc23

Printed in the United States of America.

Cover art by Zachariah James Stuef.

Dedicated to my best poetry, Riley and Clarissa

CONTENTS

FOREWORD

To be perfectly candid, I have never searched libraries or perused bookstores for books of seventeenth-century poetry. It's not that I am unfamiliar with poetry, the era, or many of its authors, but my academic work typically has me focused in other eras and subjects. It took a gentle nudge for me to take a closer look once again. I am grateful that Dr. Kerri Tom provided the impetus.

Having served with her at Concordia University Irvine for many years, I know Dr. Tom as an excellent professor, a champion of the liberal arts, and a proponent of the natural interaction of the Christian faith and academics. Benefitting from her clarity of thought and expression, countless students have come away from her engaging teaching with a broader view of the world through literature. As a colleague, I am grateful for her interdisciplinarity which has enriched our academic community. Since my theological work has a strong literary dimension, we easily found an academic affinity. She has graciously and helpfully reviewed my writing over the years, and I was fortunate to be in dialog with her as she wrote this book.

The temptation of our age is to relegate poetry to the past—either as an artifact of fading history, or as a memory of a literature class where once we were compelled to study a

really a longing to recapture what they actually had: time to reflect and learn with a respected mentor. Yet those benefits are not locked away in the past. *Be Thou My Song* provides just such an opportunity. It is an invitation to Dr. Tom's classroom where, without the pressures or distractions that may have affected us in earlier times, we can once again join in the great conversation. Here we can listen and reflect with Spenser, Milton, Donne, Herbert, Bradstreet, and Taylor, guided by Dr. Tom, contribute our own voices, and, above all, listen to the voice of a gracious God who is reflected in these works.

Steven P. Mueller, PhD
Professor of Theology,
Vice President and Chief Mission Officer
Concordia University Irvine

FOREWORD

To be perfectly candid, I have never searched libraries or perused bookstores for books of seventeenth-century poetry. It's not that I am unfamiliar with poetry, the era, or many of its authors, but my academic work typically has me focused in other eras and subjects. It took a gentle nudge for me to take a closer look once again. I am grateful that Dr. Kerri Tom provided the impetus.

Having served with her at Concordia University Irvine for many years, I know Dr. Tom as an excellent professor, a champion of the liberal arts, and a proponent of the natural interaction of the Christian faith and academics. Benefitting from her clarity of thought and expression, countless students have come away from her engaging teaching with a broader view of the world through literature. As a colleague, I am grateful for her interdisciplinarity which has enriched our academic community. Since my theological work has a strong literary dimension, we easily found an academic affinity. She has graciously and helpfully reviewed my writing over the years, and I was fortunate to be in dialog with her as she wrote this book.

The temptation of our age is to relegate poetry to the past—either as an artifact of fading history, or as a memory of a literature class where once we were compelled to study a seemingly archaic form. Yet it is so much more. Poetry is creation. It brings words to life and order from chaos. It dances between ideas demanding precise and accurate expression and the creation and celebration of beauty through imagination and language itself. The discipline of working in a particular form, of meter, structure, and the limits these demand forces the writer to use the utmost care and selectivity to say precisely what is meant. The depth of reflection and artisanship required yields something new: a meaning far deeper than the few words that it encompasses seem to indicate, and beauty that transcends a mere summary of content to lift the reader's enjoyment and understanding.

The careful labor of the poet provides riches to the reader who is willing to engage, for it makes demands of the reader as well. Reading must slow. Do not merely consume words looking for the base meaning alone, but ponder, savor, and delight in them. In a world of fast-paced momentary consumption, such reflection can be a welcome respite.

This book focuses on a narrow, but fertile swath of poetry: Christian poetry in the seventeenth century. This post-Reformation era contains treasures that reflect the hallmarks of the Reformation: in scriptural categories, these poets reveal God's grace and his gift of faith in Christ Jesus. *Sola Scriptura. Sola Gratia. Sola Fide. Solus Christus.* Indeed, this rich era of religious poetry in English is worthy of our attention and reflection.

Having served many years as a professor, I often encounter older alumni who express their regret that they did not make the most of the opportunities they had to learn and be mentored by their professors. Often, I think these regrets are

Chapter One

AN INTRODUCTION TO POETRY

C hildren love poetry.

From Mother Goose to Dr. Seuss, children are delighted by the sounds of words—how they rhyme, how they alliterate, how they convey nonsense, and how they evoke emotion. From *Goodnight Moon* to *Horton Hears a Who!*, children travel the paths where poetry guides them, often memorizing the lines long before they learn to read.

But as children go through elementary school, they encounter poetry less and less frequently as picture books are replaced with chapter books. And when they take English courses in high school and read poems again, those poems are often presented like frogs laid out for dissection where an over-analysis of the language leaves little room for enjoyment.

This is a terrible shame. Poetry, in its wide variety of forms, is an ancient art form that began as an oral tradition, a means by which a culture was kept vibrant and alive through the singing, chanting, or reciting of religious beliefs and historical events. Poetry predates literacy and requires no physical tools to be handed down from generation to generation. Imagine if all the written copies of Psalm 23 were to vanish from the earth—would Psalm 23 itself be lost? No, because so many people of faith have stored this poem in their memories and could share it over and over again.

Those of us who read the Bible are, in fact, exposed to poetry in ways that others are not, and we should rejoice in this beautiful gift from God. The Book of Psalms alone provides us with 150 lyric poems. Prophecies, lamentations, joyous hymns and songs of praise are found throughout Scripture, expressing ideas and emotions that cannot be confined to prose. And this poetry is spoken or sung by every sort of person, from the palace of King David to the humble home of the Virgin Mary.

It makes sense that if the Word of God so often takes poetic form, then the people of God, in post-Biblical times, should use poetry to express their faith. This is certainly true in medieval and Renaissance Europe, perhaps the greatest example being Dante's *Divine Comedy*, an epic that describes heaven and hell but which is really about its author's return to faith. In a recent article entitled "Christianity and Poetry," Dana Gioia traces this history of Christian poetry, noting that the "seventeenth century is the greatest period of religious poetry in English."[1] Between the poets living in England itself and those who emigrated to the American colonies, the quality and quantity of faith-based poems blossomed and flourished in new and beautiful ways.

> It makes sense that if the Word of God so often takes poetic form, then the people of God, in post-Biblical times, should use poetry to express their faith.

Be Thou My Song is both the title of this book and a line from seventeenth-century poet Edward Taylor. In his meditation on Philippians 2:9,

---

[1] Dana Gioia, "Christianity and Poetry," First Things, August 2022. https://www.firstthings.com/Article/2022/08/christianity-and-poetry.

Taylor finds that his ability to compose poetry falls short of his desire to glorify God, so he prays, "That I thy glorious Praise may Trumpet right, / Be thou my Song, and make Lord, mee thy Pipe." In one way or another, all of the poets included in the following chapters strive to convey their wonder for God's unending grace and mercy in their own limited ways; He provides the content, the song, while the writers are merely the conduits, the pipe. By reading these poems carefully, we can share in their gratitude for how God cares for us, both here on earth and in our final heavenly home.

In each chapter you will find a poem, presented in its entirety, followed by an exploration of that poem and some questions to contemplate afterwards. It is my hope that after you have read each chapter and answered the questions, you will then re-read the poem with a deeper appreciation, a deeper understanding, and a deeper love of what each poet has given to us.

> *In one way or another, all of the poets included in the following chapters strive to convey their wonder for God's unending grace and mercy in their own limited ways; He provides the content, the song, while the writers are merely the conduits, the pipe.*

****

Poetry does differ from prose, although those differences can be difficult to define along hard and fast lines. When reading poetry from the seventeenth century, we should be aware of four key elements:

3

1. *The sounds of words.* The majority of poets in this time period (with the rather notable exception of John Milton in *Paradise Lost*) use rhyme. Rhyme schemes (predictable patterns of where the rhymes will appear) vary greatly, from the simplest couplets (lines 1 and 2 rhyme, lines 3 and 4 rhyme, and so forth) to more experimental patterns (see, for example, *Amoretti* 68 in Chapter Nine). Rhyme aids in memorization. In addition to utilizing words that share sounds, the poets sometimes use words that sound alike in order to create puns, such as with *sun* and *son*.

2. *Meter.* English is a stressed language, meaning that when we speak we put emphasis on some words—and, within words, some syllables—rather than on others. For example, in the sentence, "We finished our dinner in the park," the natural stress falls on the "fin" of "finished," the "din" of "dinner," and "park." Poets make use of the natural stresses by ordering them in predictable patterns or meter. The most common pattern in spoken English—and therefore in English poetry—is the iamb. An iamb is one unstressed syllable followed by one stressed syllable, such as "to be," "the Lord," "believed." (For contrast, "corner," "fragrant," "down in" are not iambs because the stress or emphasis falls on the first syllable.) Iambs can run across words, such as in "amazing grace," where the "ing" is the unstressed syllable before the stressed "grace." Although there are other stress patterns available to poets, the iamb leads the way.

Poets then choose how many stresses—or beats—they want in each line of poetry. This tends to be three to five per line, but not every line need have the same number of beats. For example, in "Faith" in Chapter Four, George Herbert uses four beats in lines 1 and 4 of each stanza, but five beats in lines 2 and 3. Three beats per line is called *trimeter*, four is *tetrameter*, and five is *pentameter*. A regular meter also aids in memorization.

3. *Punctuation*. The same rules of punctuation apply to poetry as they do to prose, but new readers of poetry sometimes forget this when it comes to the end of a line. There are only two types of poetic lines: end-stopped and enjambed. An end-stopped line is one that ends with any type of punctuation, such as a comma, a period, a question mark, an exclamation point, a semi-colon, etc. When one reads an end-stopped line aloud, the natural pause caused by the punctuation coincides with the pause implied by the end of the line, so the reader has no difficulty in reading the line correctly. An enjambed line has no punctuation, however, but the reader may pause anyway, causing confusion. For example, let's look at the first four lines of one of John Donne's sonnets:

> At the round earth's imagined corners, blow
> Your trumpets, angels, and arise, arise
> From death, you numberless infinities
> Of souls, and to your scattered bodies go,

Lines 1, 2, and 3 are enjambed; if one pauses after "blow," "arise," and "infinities," the phrases are cut in two and become almost meaningless. Instead, punctuation needs to take precedence over line breaks, so that "blow your trumpets," "arise from death," and "infinities of souls" carry their full meaning.

5

4. *Similes and metaphors.* Similes and metaphors are comparisons between seemingly unlike things. We need go no further than the Song of Solomon 4:2: "Thy teeth are like a flock of sheep that are even shorn." In reality, teeth are nothing like sheep, but the poet uses the simile to convey something to the reader in a unique and thought-provoking way. How are teeth like a flock of shorn sheep? They are white and clean and plentiful. Could the poet have simply stated that fact? Yes, but the simile of the sheep adds a new image, an image of health and wealth. This is what metaphors and similes do: they add meaning, a deeper understanding, to what is being described. When describing similes and metaphors, we use two specific terms: *tenor* and *vehicle. Tenor* refers to the actual thing being described whereas *vehicle* refers to the object of comparison. In the example from Song of Solomon, "teeth" is the *tenor* and "flock of sheep" is the *vehicle.*

****

The six Christian poets represented in the following chapters were all motivated by their faith in their Savior to write, collectively, hundreds of poems in gratitude for the many, many gifts that He had bestowed upon them. These poems often read like, and indeed were, prayers, many of which were never intended for publication. But published they were, and they now stand as witnesses to us of God's bountiful grace, forgiveness of sins, and sure promises of eternal life.

> These poems now stand as witnesses to us of God's bountiful grace, forgiveness of sins, and sure promises of eternal life.

Chapter Two

"MAY 13, 1657"
BY ANNE BRADSTREET

I n a number of ways, Anne Bradstreet (1612-1672) was a typical woman of her time: a dutiful daughter, a devoted wife, and a loving mother. In rather significant ways, however, she lived an extraordinary life, following her father and husband to the new world in 1630 as a member of the Puritan community fleeing England, a country that they loved but which was falling further and further away—as they saw it— from the true Christian church. What distinguishes Bradstreet even more is that despite the hardships incumbent on raising a family of eight children in a foreign and dangerous land, she still found the time and the energy to produce poetry of the highest quality, ranging from a learned dialogue between Old England and New England to private love songs for her traveling husband. When her brother-in-law introduced her poetry to England, her skill as a writer and her evident learning garnered her the title of "The Tenth Muse"; in a field dominated by men, she became the first important poet of colonial America.

Many of her poems reveal her faith; as she describes her goal in "Contemplations," a lengthy poem in which she describes the beauty of God's creation and the relative insignificance of human accomplishment: "My humble eyes to lofty skies I reared / To sing some song, … / My great Creator I would magnify" (*ll.* 53-55). One of these songs is "May 13, 1657":

> As spring the winter doth succeed
> And leaves the naked trees do dress,
> The earth all black is clothed in green.
> At sunshine each their joy express.
>
> My sun's returned with healing wings,
> My soul and body doth rejoice,
> My heart exults and praises sings
> To Him that heard my wailing voice.
>
> My winter's past, my storms are gone,
> And former clouds seem now all fled,
> But if they must eclipse again,
> I'll run where I was succored.
>
> I have a shelter from the storm,
> A shadow from the fainting heat,
> I have access unto His throne,
> Who is a God so wondrous great.
>
> O hath Thou made my pilgrimage
> Thus pleasant, fair, and good,
> Blessed me in youth and elder age,
> My Baca made a springing flood.
>
> O studious am what I shall do
> To show my duty with delight;

All I can give is but Thine own
And at the most a simple mite.

The primary theme of this poem, as revealed in a diary entry, is thankfulness to God for "healing" for "a sore sickness and weakness ... which hath by fits lasted all this spring till this 11, May" ("May 11, 1657"). There is a sense of spontaneity in this poem, as the joy felt in the opening stanza finds a myriad of ways to express itself through poetic images. Bradstreet uses iambic tetrameter and a standard *abab* rhyme scheme (lines 1 and 3 of each stanza rhyme, as do lines 2 and 4) that line up well with her simple theme. But even amidst these poetic conventions, the language, metaphors, and similes are rich in meaning.

The first stanza gives us an extended simile using the metaphor of "dress" and "clothed" to describe the annual re-greening of the natural world each spring. What was "naked" and cold is now covered and warm. Since spring *always* follows winter, Bradstreet implies that whatever the subject of her simile is, it, too, was to be expected; in other words, whatever her "winter" was, spring was sure to follow. That "spring" is identified as the One who "heard my wailing voice" in stanza two, the stanza that completes the opening simile:

Simile (or vehicle)	Subject (or tenor)
Spring and sunshine	God
Naked trees and black earth	Bradstreet's soul and body

The image of God here is a bit confused, as He is her "sun" but has "healing wings." This image is a direct allusion to

9

Malachi 4:2: "But unto you that fear my name shall the Sun of righteousness arise with healing in his wings; and ye shall go forth, and grow up as calves of the stall."[1] This biblical mixed metaphor conveys a sense of something on high coming down to the speaker to give her new life. And just as the earth expresses its "joy," Bradstreet's "soul and body doth rejoice," singing "praises" in place of "wailing."

The poet may be implying that other winters have come before (we know that she often suffered serious illnesses, both before and after her voyage to the New World), but that God, like the springtime sun, has faithfully healed her each time. And, as we see in the third stanza, she foresees a repetition of this pattern; "I'll run where I was succored" informs the reader that God's protective powers will not decay with time. After all, her storms were merely "clouds," insubstantial forms that may "eclipse" the sun but never truly extinguish it.

Bradstreet shifts away from the motif of winter and spring as she notes, "I have a shelter from the storm, / A shadow from the fainting heat." By bringing in "heat," she adds summer to her calendar, demonstrating that her Lord provides for her in all seasons. This is a common image in Scripture as we read in Isaiah 25:4: " For thou hast been a strength to the poor, a strength to the needy in his distress, a refuge from the storm, a shadow from the heat, when the blast of the terrible ones is as a storm against the wall." Elsewhere, Isaiah writes, "And there shall be a tabernacle for a shadow in the day time from the heat,

---

[1] Throughout this book, I will be using the King James translation of the Bible. Although this was not the only English translation available to these authors, it was certainly the most popular and remains very much in use today for its beauty.

and for a place of refuge, and for a covert from storm and from rain" (4:6), created by God. What was true for God's people in the deserts of the Middle East is equally true for Bradstreet in the tempests of New England. She imagines this shelter as being no less than "His throne."

She then addresses God directly, acknowledging His hand in the blessing of her "pilgrimage," a term that carried special weight for the Puritans who had traversed the Atlantic to reach Massachusetts Bay Colony. She references both her "youth and elder age," again reinforcing His faithfulness towards her throughout her lifetime. He has made her "Baca ... a springing flood," recalling the beauties of Psalm 84:

> Blessed are they that dwell in thy house: they will be still praising thee.
>
> Blessed is the man whose strength is in thee; in whose heart are the ways of them.
>
> Who passing through the valley of Baca make it a well; the rain also filleth the pools.
>
> They go from strength to strength, every one of them in Zion appeareth before God.

Here, she envisions her pilgrimage, not from the Old World to the New, but from the earth to the courts of the Lord. Her physical healing is a type of the eternal healing her soul and body will experience in His house.

Although she describes God as a monarch on a throne, as "wondrous great," she uses the pronoun "Thou" rather than "You" to address Him. This is language that we associate with the King James' Bible, but we may not be aware of why it is used since it is no longer a part of our modern English. However old-fashioned and formal *thou, thee, thy,* and *thine* may sound to us, they actually point to a personal relationship between the speaker and the listener. *Thou* is the equivalent to *tu* in French or *tú* in Spanish. These personal pronouns express less formality, not more. Thus, Bradstreet has personal "access unto His throne" as she is known by Him.

She finishes her poem by wishing to show her "duty with delight" but must admit that she has very little to offer: "All I can give is but Thine own / And at the most a simple mite," alluding directly to the Widow of Mark 12:41-44:

> And Jesus sat over against the treasury, and beheld how the people cast money into the treasury: and many that were rich cast in much. And there came a certain poor widow, and she threw in two mites, which make a farthing. And he called unto him his disciples, and saith unto them, Verily I say unto you, That this poor widow hath cast more in, than all they which have cast into the treasury: For all they did cast in of their abundance; but she of her want did cast in all that she had, even all her living.

In Bradstreet's case, the "mite" is not money but the poem itself, her offering of all she has. This poem and, indeed, her ability to write poetry are gifts from God Himself, just as are all the blessings of her life. The "delight" she feels in thanking Him through poetry is yet another gift that God bestows on her, a delight that we, as her readers, are blessed to share.

Questions for Contemplation

1. What is your *mite*, your gift from God, which you delight in returning to Him and to others?

2. How has God provided shelter for you through your winters and storms?

3. Bradstreet made time to write poetry in an era free of modern-day conveniences. How might you make time for your relationship with Christ?

Chapter Three

"UPON THE BURNING OF OUR HOUSE" BY ANNE BRADSTREET

A nne Bradstreet's tone of gratitude is easy enough for us to understand in "May 13, 1657"; after all, God has blessed her with healing after a long and tiresome illness, returning her to a springtime of health and joy. Given the lack of medical treatment in New England in the seventeenth century, Bradstreet's poem of thanksgiving seems a natural response to her miraculous recovery. What we may find surprising is that she is able to feel such gratitude some nine years later in a much darker and potentially devastating circumstance, that of the destruction of her home and belongings in a housefire. "Upon the Burning of Our House July 10th, 1666" gives us a vivid description of that loss, Bradstreet's brooding over it, but also her realization that her lost wealth pales in comparison with what God has in store for her.

The poem can be broken down, roughly, into four sections: (1) the night of the fire (*lines* 1-12); (2) Bradstreet's initial response (*lines* 13-20); (3) a list of what has been lost (*lines* 21-36); and (4) Bradstreet's coming to terms with this loss (*lines* 37-54). Although the poem itself is not separated into stanzas, it is presented here with breaks for easy reference:

In silent night when rest I took
For sorrow near I did not look
I wakened was with thund'ring noise
And piteous shrieks of dreadful voice.
That fearful sound of "Fire!" and "Fire!"
Let no man know is my desire.
I, starting up, the light did spy,
And to my God my heart did cry
To strengthen me in my distress
And not to leave me succorless.
Then, coming out, beheld a space
The flame consume my dwelling place.

And when I could no longer look,
I blest His name that gave and took,
That laid my goods now in the dust.
Yea, so it was, and so 'twas just.
It was His own, it was not mine,
Far be it that I should repine;
He might of all justly bereft
But yet sufficient for us left.

When by the ruins oft I past
My sorrowing eyes aside did cast,
And here and there the places spy
Where oft I sat and long did lie:
Here stood that trunk, and there that chest,
There lay that store I counted best.
My pleasant things in ashes lie,
And them behold no more shall I.
Under thy roof no guest shall sit,
Nor at thy table eat a bit.

16

No pleasant tale shall e'er be told,
Nor things recounted done of old.
No candle e'er shall shine in thee,
Nor bridegroom's voice e'er heard shall be.
In silence ever shalt thou lie,
Adieu, Adieu, all's vanity.

Then straight I 'gin my heart to chide,
And did thy wealth on earth abide?
Didst fix thy hope on mold'ring dust?
The arm of flesh didst make thy trust?
Raise up thy thoughts above the sky
That dunghill mists away may fly.
Thou hast an house on high erect,
Framed by that mighty Architect,
With glory richly furnished,
Stands permanent though this be fled.
It's purchased and paid for too
By Him who hath enough to do.
A price so vast as is unknown
Yet by His gift is made thine own;
There's wealth enough, I need no more,
Farewell, my pelf, farewell my store.
The world no longer let me love,
My hope and treasure lies above.

The poem opens with the confusion of sounds and sights that awakened Bradstreet on that dreadful night. What, indeed, could be more "fearful" than "shrieks" of "Fire!"? Where she had sought "rest," she discovers "noise"; although she neither looked for "sorrow" nor desired catastrophe, they come upon her in the night. Escaping without personal injury, she still must watch "flame consume my dwelling place." One can only imagine the terror of such an event.

Yet, in the middle of this chaos, we hear another "cry" as Bradstreet calls to her God for strength and succor. The clouds she had described in "May 13, 1657" have returned; in that poem, she had said, "But if they must eclipse again, / I'll run where I was succored," and that is exactly what she does here, seeking relief where she has found it before, knowing He will not leave her "succorless." Furthermore, because she identifies Him as "my God," we see the relationship between them—whereas anyone might call on a generic God in an emergency, she calls on *her* God and she calls from her "heart."

Still, it is painful for her to watch the fire, so she averts her eyes and contemplates what has transpired. She acknowledges three key points in this section: (1) that since God "gave" her her "goods," those goods were on loan to her, as a steward, so to speak, and belonged to the giver; (2) that if God allowed the housefire, it must be "just" and according to His will; and (3) that God could have taken more (including human lives) but left "sufficient" for her. Therefore, she should refrain from repining, from feeling any unhappiness or expressing such unhappiness aloud.

Yet this sort of pat answer ("the Lord hath given, and the Lord hath taken it" [Job 1:21]) is not enough to comfort Bradstreet as time passes and as she walks by the "ruins" of her home, the continual reminder of that which is no more. This section of the poem is indeed "sorrowing" as she recounts her losses. Although she mentions material goods such as a "trunk," a "chest," and her "pleasant things," the real sadness is for things more ephemeral than those. These are the things that distinguish a home from merely a house.

As Bradstreet eyes the ruins, she speaks directly to the home that exists only in her memory: "Under thy roof no guest shall sit, / Nor at thy table eat a bit." In this, she both remembers times past and envisions times that will not come, both memory and imagination focused on the unnamed "guest." The Christian virtue of hospitality has been denied her as she has no home to share with others, no place in which to break bread, no way of offering rest to a weary traveler.

The next loss may include that guest, but seems to gather in a whole family of listeners: "No pleasant tale shall e'er be told, / Nor things recounted done of old." Here, the idea of conversation over a meal is widened out to include both new tales never heard before and the sorts of reminiscences common to large families. There is a sense of conviviality lost, of community silenced, of oral treasures never to be shared. In an age where books are rare and expensive, and modern forms of media are completely unknown, such spoken tales are truly invaluable, especially to people living on the edge of civilization.

Whereas the "guest" and tales speak to a wider sense of communal connection, the final loss seems to be the most intimate, the most personal to Bradstreet as she remarks, "No candle e'er shall shine in thee, / Nor bridegroom's voice e'er heard shall be." Her husband was often away from home, as attested to in poems such as "A Letter to Her Husband, Absent Upon Public Employment," and we can imagine the candle, lit by Anne herself, as she awaited the return of her beloved bridegroom. Beyond its role as rest for wanderers and gathering place for family, the now-burned home was the site of many happy reunions between husband and wife. But now it lies in "silence."

There is no denying the heartfelt emotion of this section as Bradstreet comes close to being overwhelmed by grief for what she has lost. Yet for all she may remember, she sees before her "mold'ring dust," the ashes of her "wealth on earth," and she chastises herself for thinking that her "hope" and "trust" were in such "dunghill mists," the air rising from excrement. She now raises her thoughts, lifting them to her real hope and trust. Instead of focusing on God as a giver and taker, as she had done before, Bradstreet sees Him as the greatest giver of all.

This time, He is described as the "mighty Architect" who has built a "permanent" house for her, unlike the one that is gone. Like St. Paul, she acknowledges "that if our earthly house of this tabernacle were dissolved, we have a building of God, a house not made with hands, eternal in the heavens" (2 Cor. 5:1). Bradstreet also seems to be referencing Christ's words to His disciples: "In my Father's house are many dwelling places: if it were not so, I would have told you: I go to prepare a place for you" (John 14:2). Furthermore, this heavenly dwelling is "purchased and paid for too / By Him who hath enough to do"; the poem links the permanent home to the "inheritance, for the redemption of that liberty purchased unto the praise of his glory" (Eph. 1:14) that Christ achieved for us on the cross. The difference between earthly wealth and "His gift" is the focus, just as it is in 1 Peter 1:18-19: "Knowing that ye were not redeemed with corruptible things, as silver and gold, …

But with the precious blood of Christ, as of a Lamb undefiled, and without spot."

It is in understanding this "price so vast" that Bradstreet is able to bid "farewell" to what she has lost in the fire, to turn away from the ruins in front of her and towards the heavenly home she now envisions; the poem concludes with "My hope and treasure lies above." And although she doesn't state it directly, we can find a further hint about what she will experience in heaven if we return for a moment to her list of losses. As stated above, the loss of the "bridegroom's voice" is a deeply felt one; the use of the term "bridegroom" for her husband of many years speaks to the joy of the bride on her wedding day while simultaneously uniting the "bride" and the "groom" in one term. But there is another reason for using "bridegroom" in this context. Christ Himself is seen as the Bridegroom, coming to His church, His Bride; Bradstreet uses this image in "As Weary Pilgrim," where she prepares herself for the grave: "Lord make me ready for that day, / Then come, dear Bridegroom, come away." By using "bridegroom" in the center of "Upon the Burning of Our House," she subtly points to the Bridegroom—her "hope and treasure"—whose voice will be heard in her—and our—eternal home.

Questions for Contemplation

1. Where do your hope and treasure lie? How does that affect your attitude toward material possessions?

2. How might Bradstreet's words comfort you during a time of loss?

3. Which Christian virtues do you wish to share in your home?

Chapter Four

"FAITH"
BY GEORGE HERBERT

Although Anne Bradstreet's primary source of literary inspiration for her religious poetry was her Bible, the poetry of British Protestant writers was available to her as well. George Herbert (1593-1633), a quiet country rector who wrote poetry for his own spiritual growth, found unexpected fame after his death. His book of devotional poems, *The Temple*, was published in 1633 in England and quickly established itself as a popular work among Anglicans and Puritans alike. Such popularity may have been due to the lyrics' unique combination of utter honesty with a distinct playfulness of expression. In other words, Herbert is extremely serious about his faith in, and relationship with, God, yet he demonstrates a willingness to experiment with the language and the format of his poems in his attempts to describe that faith in new and affecting ways. He is especially fascinated with how metaphors—both those of biblical origin and new ones taken from his own time and place— might be used in this endeavor.

> Herbert is extremely serious about his faith in, and relationship with, God, yet he demonstrates a willingness to experiment with the language and the format of his poems in his attempts to describe that faith in new and affecting ways.

Herbert's poem, "Faith," uses a series of metaphors in an exploration of how faith saves him:

> Lord, how couldst thou so much appease
> Thy wrath for sin as, when man's sight was dim,
> And could see little, to regard his ease,
> > And bring by Faith all things to him?

> Hungry I was, and had no meat:
> I did conceit a most delicious feast;
> I had it straight, and did as truly eat,
> > As ever did a welcome guest.

> There is a rare outlandish root,
> Which when I could not get, I thought it here:
> That apprehension cured so well my foot,
> > That I can walk to heav'n well near.

> I owed thousands and much more:
> I did believe that I did nothing owe,
> And liv'd accordingly; my creditor
> > Believes so too, and lets me go.

> Faith makes me anything, or all
> That I believe is in the sacred story:
> And where sin placeth me in Adam's fall,
> > Faith sets me higher in his glory.

> If I go lower in the book,
> What can be lower than the common manger?
> Faith puts me there with him, who sweetly took
> > Our flesh and frailty, death and danger.

If bliss had lien in art or strength,
None but the wise or strong had gain'd it:
Where now by Faith all arms are of a length;
    One size doth all conditions fit.

A peasant may believe as much
As a great clerk, and reach the highest stature.
Thus dost thou make proud knowledge bend and crouch
    While grace fills up uneven nature.

When creatures had no real light
Inherent in them, thou didst make the sun,
Impute a lustre, and allow them bright;
    And in this show, what Christ hath done.

That which before was dark'ned clean
With bushy groves, pricking the looker's eye,
Vanisht away, when Faith did change the scene:
    And then appear'd a glorious sky.

What though my body run to dust?
Faith cleaves unto it, counting ev'ry grain
With an exact and most particular trust,
    Reserving all for flesh again.

This poem, like many of Herbert's, is addressed directly to
God, beginning with a question that gets directly to the heart of
the matter: given the enormity of mankind's sin and its blind-
ness to both the sin itself and its ability to escape God's wrath,
why would God "bring by Faith all things" to mankind? Why

would He pay attention to mankind or to its relief? With these questions, Herbert makes it clear that faith does not emanate from mankind but is given by God Himself to "appease" His own anger. By capitalizing Faith, he personifies it, making it an active agent of God's will.

Mankind's helplessness to rectify its own dire situation is made more personal and more substantial in the second stanza: "Hungry I was, and had no meat." This is the first of three metaphors Herbert imagines to demonstrate the power of the Faith provided to him by God: where he is hungry, lame, and indebted, his Faith provides a "feast," a cure, and redemption. And all of these metaphors play with the biblical language associated with Christ in one way or another as He fed the hungry, cured the lame, and paid the debt of sin on our behalf.

In addition, all three metaphors involve terms of thought or understanding as Herbert shows how Faith works through the poet's mind. For example, when he "did conceit" or imagine the feast, it appeared; when he apprehended the cure, he could walk; when he "did believe" that he owed nothing, his debt disappeared. Faith—the Faith provided by the Lord—gives Herbert a sure faith in God's bounty, a sure knowledge rather than an emotion or vague feeling.

But Herbert has even more to say about Faith as a transformative gift in the believer's life. Herbert juxtaposes his rightful place in the "sin" of "Adam's fall" with his new seat in "glory," a place he can attain only through Faith. He then plays with this idea of high and low seats, and of switching between them, by noting the lowliness of "the common manger" where Christ "took / Our flesh and frailty, death and danger." But if Christ is in a low place, Herbert's "Faith puts me there with him," making the argument that the manger is both high and low—low for Christ who came down from heaven, but high for Herbert as he is now with God. Christ's descent makes possible Herbert's ascent.

As Christ came down to earth and Faith raises us up to heaven, the distance between God and mankind is eradicated. This leveling works in another way as men of different talents and social statuses are made equal through Faith. As Herbert sees it, happiness might have been given to none but "the wise or strong" if Faith had not a "one size fits all" policy. The Faith given a "peasant" is the same given "a great clerk," the former an example of illiteracy, the latter a product of a sound education. Herbert makes it clear that "grace," the undeserved gift of God, rights the "uneven" dealings of the random gifts of "nature."

In the next stanza, all humans, peasant or clerk, are "creatures," equal beings who owe their existence to the Creator. Herbert equates these creatures to the moon as they "had no real light / Inherent in them" but required "the sun" to make them bright. The "sun" / "son" pun is a favorite of Christian poets, but in case we missed it, he notes that this sun, bringing light to the creatures, shows "what Christ hath done." The brightness of His creatures merely reflects "the real light" of the savior. And just as the sun "Impute[s] a lustre" to the moon, Christ imputes His righteousness to us.

The poet proceeds to play further with images of light and dark by pointing backwards to the opening stanza where "man's sight was dim." Now, mankind's eyesight is encumbered by bushes, "pricking the looker's eye," bushes that may be related to the many thorns that beset God's people in the Old Testament, beginning with the "Thorns also and thistles" that are a result of

God's cursing the ground in Genesis 3. In any case, these prickly bushes could be any earthly impediments that separate us from the Father. Yet Faith clears away the dark bushes to reveal a new "scene," "a glorious sky." This "glorious sky" hearkens back to the "glory" where Faith had set the speaker in stanza five.

At the appearance of this "glorious sky," Herbert is comforted even as he contemplates his own mortality: "What though my body run to dust?" Instead of picturing this dust dissipating in the wind, he foresees that "Faith cleaves unto it, counting ev'ry grain / … / Reserving all for flesh again." Just as Jesus tells us in Matthew, "all the hairs of your head are numbered" (10:30), Herbert sees the care with which God will raise His children from the dust to clothe them in new bodies as prophesied in Daniel 12:2a: "And many of them that sleep in the dust of the earth shall awake, some to everlasting life."

Ultimately, Herbert's faith in forgiveness of sins and in eternal life is a direct result of God's grace in sending Faith to him despite his blindness and his debt of "thousands and much more." Although he is an heir of Adam and deserves death, he has faith because "Faith cleaves," holds tight to, his mortal dust, serving and reserving him for heavenly life. Similarly, the faith that God sends to us will bring us to everlasting life in Him.

Questions for Contemplation

1. Re-read stanza two. How does Faith feed you?

2. Re-read stanza nine. In this analogy, how are Christians like the moon?

3. Why is it so important that we understand our faith as a gift from God and not as self-generated?

Chapter Five

+————•————+

"SEPULCHRE"
BY GEORGE HERBERT

n "Faith," Herbert demonstrates his poetic playfulness by using a number of varied metaphors to describe how Faith has saved him, ranging from a feast to a cure to a debt paid to a sky cleared of darkness. In "Sepulchre," the approach is quite different: instead of using different metaphors to describe the same spiritual reality, he uses the central image of a stone in a variety of ways, both literal and metaphorical, to communicate, in some surprising ways, the love of Christ for His people.

The poem is addressed to Christ's dead body on the occasion of its burial on Good Friday:

> O Blessed body! Whither art thou thrown?
> No lodging for thee, but a cold hard stone?
> So many hearts on earth, and yet not one
> Receive thee?
>
> Sure there is room within our hearts good store;
> For they can lodge transgressions by the score:
> Thousands of toys dwell there, yet out of door
> They leave thee.

But that which shows them large, shows them unfit.
Whatever sin did this pure rock commit,
Which holds thee now? Who hath indicted it
        Of murder?

Where our hard hearts have took up stones to
    brain thee,
And missing this, most falsely did arraign thee;
Only these stones in quiet entertain thee,
        And order.

And as of old, the law by heav'nly art
Was writ in stone; so thou, which also art
The letter of the word, find'st no fit heart
        To hold thee.

Yet do we still persist as we began,
And so should perish, but that nothing can,
Though it be cold, hard, foul, from loving man
        Withhold thee.

The very first line of the poem is designed to shock the reader with its stark contrast between the "Blessed body" of Christ—a body that is holy and worthy of veneration—and its treatment as it is "thrown" into the sepulchre of the title, tossed away as if it has no value. "Thrown" seems to be an ironic pun on "throne," where Christ's body should be seated. This "cold hard stone" is further contrasted with the "hearts on earth" that do not "Receive" Him. The brilliance of this opening stanza is how deftly Herbert moves from the literal "stone" to the stony hearts that he will describe more fully further on. Again,

Herbert uses a subtle irony by asking why the very persons for whom Christ died will not accept Him, not even one, reminding us of Romans 3:10: "There is none righteous, no, not one."

Herbert then argues for the capaciousness of the human heart, noting that there is plenty of room for "transgressions by the score" and "Thousands of toys." In Matthew 15:19, Christ Himself provides a list of such transgressions, telling His disciples, "For out of the heart come evil thoughts, murders, adulteries, fornications, thefts, false testimonies, slanders." As for "toys," they are not necessarily sinful; they are not so much childish (as the word connotes today) as they are foolish, frivolous, or nonsensical. Stocked with such evil and worthless items, the human heart has no room for Christ's crucified body and all the significance that it carries with it.

Despite its being "large," the human heart is "unfit" for Christ in comparison to the physical sepulchre. That rock is "pure" and without "sin," a description equally apt for its occupant. When Herbert asks, "Who hath indicted it / Of murder?" the question is rhetorical, reflecting not on the grave but on those hearts filled with sins: as Jesus tells us in Matthew 5:21-22, murder in the heart is equal to murder of the body and deserving of equal punishment.

But the following stanza reminds us that the human heart is capable of actual murder, and the victim is Christ Himself. Failing to stone Him to death (John 8:59—"Then they took up stones to cast at him: but Jesus hid himself ..."), the Jewish people of Christ's time "falsely" brought Him to trial so that the Romans might crucify Him. By using the phrase, "our hard hearts have took up stones," Herbert aligns himself and his own people with those persons described in the Gospels who participated in the death of Christ, showing that *all* people are equally guilty of killing Christ. In fact, no human would be able to "entertain," to welcome or to be hospitable towards Him; He can only lie in "quiet" among the stones of a graveyard.

This situation seems to leave Herbert with an unsolvable problem. He remembers that "the law by heav'nly art / Was writ in stone," referring to Deuteronomy 4:13 where the Lord gave His laws to Moses: "And he declared unto you his covenant, which he commanded you to perform, even ten commandments; and he wrote them upon two tables of stone." Likewise, Christ who is the "letter of the word" should be inscribed, yet there is "no fit heart / To hold" Him. We know from John 1 that Christ *is* the Word, but by calling Him the "letter of the word," Herbert seems to be implying that He is a sort of epistle, carrying the Word of God into our hearts.

Yet the problem remains—how can the Word enter hearts that "persist" in their hardness, that have no room for Christ? In the final stanza, Herbert leaves no doubt that these hearts are "cold, hard, [and] foul" and, left on their own, they would inevitably "perish." Their fate would be an eternal sepulchre, the punishment they so abundantly deserve. Therefore, the solution can *only* come from Jesus, for "nothing can" "Withhold" Him "from loving man." By His death, burial, and resurrection, Christ overcomes our cold hearts and our deserved death.

If we return to the first stanza and its opening questions, we see a clearer answer. It is precisely because "not one" of the "many hearts on earth" would or could "Receive" Christ that He died and was buried in "a cold hard stone." By choosing such a sepulchre, He took our place there, and just as the stone rolled in front of His tomb could not hold Him in, our stony hearts cannot "Withhold" Him from saving us.

Questions for Contemplation

1. What "toys" dwell in your heart which push Jesus aside?
2. How might you use this poem in a prayer of confession?
3. Why is it important for you, as it was for Herbert, to see yourself in the murderous hearts of Jesus' time?

Chapter Six

+————————•————————+

"THE ELIXIR"
BY GEORGE HERBERT

lthough George Herbert was quite adept at playing with biblical imagery and metaphors, manipulating the language in new ways to find fuller expression of his deep relationship with his Lord, he delighted also in using more contemporary objects in his devotional poetry. A quick glace through *The Temple*'s table of contents gives us titles such as "The Pulley," "The Bag," and "The Water-course," a poem about plumbing and repentance. Near the end of the collection comes "The Elixir," which links a variety of images, ranging from "drudgery" to alchemy, to explore the concept of vocation.

In Herbert's day, *elixir* had a narrower meaning than it has today and was directly linked to alchemy and the "science" of turning inferior metals into gold. As an offshoot of this miraculous property, elixirs were also a source of prolonging life. By the second half of Herbert's life, medieval notions of the miraculous possibilities of alchemy were fast being replaced with more practical notions of chemistry, so titling a devotional lyric "Elixir" would have wrinkled a few brows in consternation, especially since the word itself does not appear in the King James Bible. Nor does it appear in the poem itself:

Teach me, my God and King,
In all things thee to see,
And what I do in anything,
To do it as for thee:

Not rudely, as a beast,
To run into an action;
But still to make thee prepossess'd,
And give it his perfection.

A man that looks on glass,
On it may stay his eye;
Or if he pleaseth, through it pass,
And then the heav'n espy.

All may of thee partake:
Nothing can be so mean,
Which with his tincture (for thy sake)
Will not grow bright and clean.

A servant with this clause
Makes drudgery divine:
Who sweeps a room, as for thy laws,
Makes that and th'action fine.

This is the famous stone
That turneth all to gold:
For that which God doth touch and own
Cannot for less be told.

This poem opens simply enough with a direct appeal from
Herbert to his Lord: "Teach me." From the outset, the speaker

presents himself as someone in need of instruction in two vitally important areas: how to "see" the world around him and how to "do"—to behave once his sight has been altered. He needs to be taught how to see God in "all things" and to do "anything"—all things—as if he is doing it for God. His desire for such instruction may have been sparked by Christ's words in Matthew 25:35-40:

> "For I was an hungred, and ye gave me meat: I was thirsty, and ye gave me drink: I was a stranger, and ye took me in: Naked, and ye clothed me: I was sick, and ye visited me: I was in prison, and ye came unto me. Then shall the righteous answer him, saying, Lord, when saw we thee an hungred, and fed thee? or thirsty, and gave thee drink? When saw we thee a stranger, and took thee in? or naked, and clothed thee? Or when saw we thee sick, or in prison, and came unto thee? And the King shall answer and say unto them, Verily I say unto you, Inasmuch as ye have done it unto one of the least of these my brethren, ye have done it unto me."

Knowing he is serving Christ by caring for others will encourage Herbert to do just that.

Why he needs instruction is made clear in the next verse as Herbert describes his normal *modus operandi*: to rush into "action" "as a beast." It was typical during the Renaissance to think of a man as consisting of three parts: the body, the part linked to man's animal nature; the mind, the part linked to man's intellectual or reasonable nature; and the soul, linked to man's divine or immortal nature. Therefore, without God's instruction, Herbert's actions will be beast-like, impulsive and crude, seeking to fulfill his own physical needs and desires.

Instead, he asks God to "prepossess" his actions, to take hold of his actions or to inspire them, so that they are given "perfection." Note the shift here from being *taught* by God to being worked directly upon by Him.

The next stanza introduces a new image to illustrate the difference between the limited vision of a human being and the true vision of one taught or molded by God. Herbert describes the phenomenon of trying to look outside through a "glass" or window, only to see one's own reflection, which "stays" or stops "his eye" from looking farther. Yet if he tries, he will look past himself to see "the heav'n" beyond. This image implies that focusing on oneself impedes one from seeing the truth, the dwelling place of God. The reflection in the "glass" (a term that cleverly combines mirror and window) is but an ephemeral shadow compared to heaven. This verse may be a reference to 1 Corinthians 13:12, where St. Paul envisions a perfect future: "For now we see through a glass, darkly; but then face to face: now I know in part; but then shall I know even as also I am known." Herbert needs God's instruction to see past his own narcissistic reflection.

Herbert continues by noting that "All" may take part in God and in His vision, no matter how "mean" or lowly we may be. This is made possible by God's cleansing man's "tincture" or stain. There may be a second meaning to "tincture" here: in alchemy, a tincture is an immaterial essence that infuses a material object. In that case, "his tincture" would refer to God's entering man as the Holy Spirit. Thus we have man's sinful tincture being washed away by the infusion of God's tincture; His divine essence cleanses our sinful stain.

The result of this cleansing is worth repeating in full:

A servant with this clause
    Makes drudgery divine:
Who sweeps a room, as for thy laws,
    Makes that and th'action fine.

The lowly man, here described as a "servant" or slave, whose very work is "drudgery," now can see the divinity in it. Even the simplest act of sweeping becomes "fine" because the servant does it with a new vision, following the two greatest "laws": "Jesus said unto him, Thou shalt love the Lord thy God with all thy heart, and with all thy soul, and with all thy mind. This is the first and great commandment. And the second is like unto it, Thou shalt love thy neighbour as thyself" (Matt. 22:37-39). Sweeping the floor for one's master becomes a way to love one's neighbor; this love is at the heart of vocation.

The true value of this service is made clear in the poem's final stanza, where Herbert returns to the concept of alchemy. The fabled philosopher's "stone" that turns base metals "all to gold" is revealed to be God's "touch" that allows him to see God in "all things" and in all he does. Human attempts at alchemy, based on the material world, always fail; God is the true "Elixir" of the title, the one who gives life. Thus touched by God, Herbert demonstrates to us the true value of our vocations; sweeping the room, for neighbor and for King, is indeed golden.

Questions for Contemplation

1. Have you ever run into action without asking for God's teaching? What was the result?

2. What sorts of false "alchemy" do you sometimes pursue?

3. What "drudgery" in your life might be turned to gold by seeing it through God's word?

Chapter Seven

"DIVINE MEDITATION 1"
BY JOHN DONNE

Sixteen-thirty-three was a banner year for Protestant poetry in England. Not only was humble George Herbert's *Temple* published, but so were the collected *Poems* of the famous John Donne (1572-1631). Donne had been Dean of St. Paul's Cathedral, and his sermons were extremely popular, both in person and in printed form. His audiences often included members of the royal family.

Unlike Herbert, who wrote only devotional poetry, Donne was a master of many genres, including satires, elegies, and love poems. These poems to and about women run the gamut of emotion from deep tenderness to outright viciousness, and while some of these lyrics may be autobiographical, many are clearly flights of fancy, the poet trying on different tones and attitudes. But in his devotional poetry, we find the same honest consistency that we find in Bradstreet and in Herbert, the expression of a sinner who is wholly dependent upon the Savior for every good thing in life.

Many of these poems are referred to as "Holy Sonnets"; before we look at one closely, it is worth taking the time to understand what a sonnet is and how it was utilized before Donne.

The sonnet is a rather tidy and compact form of lyric poetry, originating in Italy, moving through France, and then finding its English version in Henry VIII's court. Its most popular authors—Petrarch in Florence and Sir Philip Sidney in London—used it to write to Laura and Stella, respectively, their ideal beautiful and virtuous women whom they loved from afar. Sidney's sonnets became so popular in the 1590s that every poet—some good, some ridiculously bad—was trying his hand at composing this fourteen-line art form, including William Shakespeare, who wrote more than 150, including his most famous sonnet, #18, "Shall I compare thee to a summer's day?"

It is not surprising, then, that Donne should write sonnets as well, but it is surprising in *how* he uses them. He never writes a love sonnet to a woman despite the facts that sonnets had become synonymous with love poetry and that Donne himself wrote many love poems. Instead, Donne writes sonnets to and about God, replacing the ideal—but ultimately fictional—woman with the only truly perfect object of love and worship.

In contrast to God's perfection, Donne describes his own sinfulness in stark and sometimes brutal terms, in full knowledge that "all have sinned, and come short of the glory of God" (Rom. 3:23). "Divine Meditation 1" explores this truth in a plea to God:

> Thou hast made me, and shall thy work decay?
> Repair me now, for now mine end doth haste,
> I run to death, and death meets me as fast,
> And all my pleasures are like yesterday,
> I dare not move my dim eyes any way,

Despair behind, and death before doth cast
Such terror, and my feeble flesh doth waste
By sin in it, which it towards hell doth weigh;
Only thou art above, and when towards thee
By thy leave I can look, I rise again;
But our old subtle foe so tempteth me,
That not one hour I can myself sustain;
Thy Grace may wing me to prevent his art,
And thou like adamant draw mine iron heart.

Donne's prayer opens with a question that acknowledges two truths that seem to contradict one another: (1) he was created by God, yet (2) he is in a state of "decay," of dissolution towards death. Such a contradiction seems, initially, like an excuse for Donne to complain, to ask, "How could you let this happen to me?" But when he tells God, "Repair me now" in the next line, the hint of complaint is replaced with an urgency for God to halt and heal the degradation that is occurring.

And why the urgency? Because, as Donne acknowledges, he "run[s] to death" as death runs towards him. This line pictures Donne and death as a pair of lovers, eager to be united, a picture that is supposed to shock us as we usually imagine death chasing us down against our will. Here, Donne confesses his own sinful life as a running after death and, as will be made clearer in line eight, after hell as well.

Despite running towards death, a movement that appears inevitable, Donne feels and fears what such a death will mean for him. Already, his "flesh" is "feeble," his "eyes" are "dim," sure signs of how his body "doth waste / By sin in it." Whatever "pleasures" his flesh may have afforded him are now as irretrievable as "yesterday." Greater than physical decay, however, is the spiritual "terror" that grips him, terror brought on not only by his mortality but by "Despair." It is despair, the complete absence of hope, that dogs him, preventing him from turning away from death.

Up until this point in the sonnet, Donne has created a sense of horizontal movement as the speaker is pursued by despair and runs towards death. But in line eight, he shifts the language to represent a vertical movement by which sin "weigh[s]" his flesh "towards hell." This is a significant move as it makes crystal clear that earthly death may result in an eternity of despair in hell. By using the word "weigh," Donne imparts the heaviness of his sin-filled body and soul.

Although he is weighed down, he "can look" to God "above." Notably, however, he cannot do this on his own but only through God's "leave," His permission. If God will have it so, Donne can look to Him and "rise again." Donne's faith is completely dependent on God's grace. Moreover, his moving up and away from hell is similarly dependent, as "rise again" points to both the current state of his soul and his future resurrection in Christ.

Donne understands that his utter dependence on God can never be replaced with his own self-reliance. When he is left on his own, the temptation to sin from Satan, his "old subtle foe," is so great "That not one hour can myself sustain" above hell; he needs God every hour of every day. Only God's "Grace may wing" him, lift him towards heaven, and "prevent" Satan's "art" or artifice, his crafty lies.

This idea of being lifted up is reinforced by the last image and the last line of the poem: "thou like adamant draw mine iron heart." Donne's iron heart reminds us of the weight of sin and also of the hard hearts of Scripture. For instance, "Zedekiah … did that which was evil in the sight of the LORD his God, … he stiffened his neck, and hardened his heart from turning unto the LORD God of Israel" (2 Chron. 36:11-13). But Donne's iron heart, heavy as it may be with sin, is drawn upward by God's "adamant," a word that has a double meaning. Its primary meaning is a magnetic stone, one that attracts Donne's iron heart. This metaphor once again demonstrates the speaker's helplessness to rise up on his own. The secondary meaning is that God is like a diamond, both in brilliance and in hardness. Donne may be implying that while his heart is as hard as iron, God's heart is even more endurable, even unbreakable.

Thus, the sonnet that began in terror and despair ends with the saving power of God's Grace. And Donne has taken the standard form of a romantic love sonnet to express God's unending love for Donne and, by extension, for all His people.

Questions for Contemplation

1. What sins seem to weigh you down more than others? How does God lift you up again?

2. Do you think that sin can "dim" your sight? What does that mean to you?

3. Donne took a popular secular form of poetry, the love sonnet, and found a higher purpose for it. Do you see artists doing this now? What is the effect of these attempts?

Chapter Eight

"A HYMN TO GOD THE FATHER" BY JOHN DONNE

S in and death are common themes in John Donne's devotional prayers. Although his most famous poem, "Death be not proud," challenges Death directly, telling it boldly, "Death thou shalt die," many of his lyrics show a real fear of death and concomitant beseeching of God for rescue, as we saw in "Divine Meditation 1." In "A Hymn to God the Father," Donne calls upon God again as he tallies up the immensity of his sins.

This hymn is presented in three numbered verses. By numbering them in this way, he encourages the reader to pause after each one, to contemplate it separately before moving on.

I
Wilt thou forgive that sin where I begun,
　　Which was my sin, though it were done before?
Wilt thou forgive that sin, through which I run,
　　And do run still: though still I do deplore?
　　When thou hast done, thou hast not done,
　　　　For, I have more.

II
Wilt thou forgive that sin which I have won
　　Others to sin? and, made my sin their door?

Wilt thou forgive that sin which I did shun
>   A year, or two: but wallowed in, a score?
>   When thou hast done, thou hast not done,
>   For I have more.

III

I have a sin of fear, that when I have spun
>   My last thread, I shall perish on the shore;
> But swear by thy self, that at my death thy son
>   Shall shine as he shines now, and heretofore;
>   And, having done that, thou hast done,
>   I fear no more.

As Donne often does, this hymn opens with a question, a question that moves in two possible directions. He asks God if He will forgive a sin that "were done before," implying that (a) it is not a new sin to Donne nor (b) a new sin in the world. By describing it is "that sin where I begun," he acknowledges that it is a very old form of sinning for him while also noting the original sin in which we all begin. This looking backward is then balanced by looking at right now where Donne "run[s] still" through this sin, even as he "deplore[s]" it; this echoes St. Paul's writing, "for what I would, that do I not; but what I hate, that do I" (Rom. 7:15b). By using the verb *run,* rather than *do,* Donne shows how active is his sin and how fully he engages in it. Finally, the stanza points to the future, for even if God forgives what has been done already, Donne has "more" sinning to come, and since the sins will keep on coming, Donne fears that God's work of forgiveness will never be completed, that he can, somehow, "out sin" God's mercy.

In the first stanza, we see Donne torn between despair and hope. On the one hand, he knows that God can and will forgive him, but, on the other hand, he knows that it is impossible for him to stop sinning, no matter how much he may wish to. By asking twice, "Wilt thou forgive that sin[?]," he is questioning God's patience with him, truly wondering if He will continue to forgive such a man as he is.

Stanza II ups the ante by identifying the types of sins that Donne commits, while asking twice more, "Wilt thou forgive that sin[?]" He confesses that his sin has "won / Others to sin" and has been a "door" that led them to sin. This is a serious confession, considering that Christ said, "Woe unto you, scribes and Pharisees, hypocrites! for ye compass sea and land to make one proselyte, and when he is made, ye make him twofold more the child of hell than yourselves" (Matt. 23:15). Given that he has caused others to sin, Donne's fear that he has sinned too heavily can be heard in his questioning.

His second question concerns a sin that he managed to "shun / A year, or two: but wallowed in, a score." A score is twenty, or ten times as many years spent in sinning than in those not. The verb *wallow* conjures up the image of a pig in mud, totally immersed in its own filth—a fitting image for the self-indulgent sinner.

He ends this second stanza exactly as he ended the first, again juxtaposing the seemingly contradictory facts that God will forgive the sins already committed but Donne has "more" to come. How can these two realities be reconciled?

The answer appears in the third and final stanza: Donne will stop sinning when he dies, when he spins his "last thread," a metaphor taken from the Fates of Greek mythology who spin out, and finally cut, each man's life. He confesses his final sin as "a sin of fear," not of dying per se but of "perish[ing] on the shore." The "shore" here may be a combination of another Greek story and of Christian imagery. Dante uses Greek mythology to create his own version of hell, as his *Inferno* recounts in Canto III:

> Thereafter all together they drew back,
> Bitterly weeping, to the accursed shore,
> Which waiteth every man who fears not God.

Conversely, John Bunyan in 1678 (about forty years after Donne passed away) has the allegorical figure of Christian pass through the river Jordan: "Christian therefore presently found ground to stand upon, and so it followed that the rest of the river was but shallow. Thus they got over" (*The Pilgrim's Progress*, p. 152). In either case, Donne imagines an endless death separate from the souls at peace if he must remain on the far shore.

To calm his fear, he asks God to "swear by thy self," to make a promise that can never be broken. Donne asks to be in the presence of Christ, that "thy son / Shall shine as he shines now," forevermore. The son / sun pun is a favorite of Christian writers, speaking to the biblical description of Jesus as "the true Light, which lighteth every man that cometh into the world" (John 1:9). If God the Father makes such an oath, then Donne's "sin of fear" will be "no more" as he will no longer question God's ability and willingness to forgive him and to keep him in His resurrection grace.

In addition to the popular son / sun pun, there is another important pun in this hymn, one that only this poet can make. The word "done" appears no less than seven times in these three stanzas, and we would be remiss if we did not hear *Donne* in these repetitions. In stanzas I and II, God has *Donne* in His hand, but the speaker fears that He has not *Donne* because of his continued sinning. But in stanza III, as God swears that the poet will be in the Savior's presence after death, he knows for certain that God has *Donne*. Thus, he can say, with confidence, "I fear no more." Even if most of us do not share the poet's surname, we can most certainly share his fearlessness in the light of God's forgiveness.

Questions for Contemplation

1. Do you ever share Donne's fear that your own sins will outpace God's forgiveness? How do we know that this is not so?

2. Donne was a renowned preacher. Do you find comfort in knowing that such a man had these problems with sinning?

3. Can you think of other ways in which the Son is like the sun? How does He outshine the sun?

Chapter Nine

·————·————·

AMORETTI 68
BY EDMUND SPENSER

The greatest Protestant poet of the Elizabethan era (1558-1603) is Edmund Spenser (1552/53-1599). Although technically not a seventeenth-century writer, his immense popularity and influence on such poets as Anne Bradstreet and John Milton warrant him a place in this little book. The difficulty, however, in presenting his work in a study such as this is that his best poems are thousands of lines long. His most famous production, an epic poem, is *The Faerie Queene* (1596), an allegorical adventure designed to model Holiness, Temperance, Chastity, Friendship, Justice, and Courtesy by embodying these Christian virtues in bold knights who defeat vices such as duplicity, sexual immorality, and unjust anger. Spenser's goal was instruction through entertainment, and *The Faerie Queene* is quite entertaining indeed, especially when the Redcrosse Knight, an ordinary man made holy by Christ's act of redemption, defeats a huge and terrifying dragon, a symbol of Satan, hell, and death.

As wonderful as it might be to share a selection of *The Faerie Queene* here, it is simply not feasible. Instead, we will look at a sonnet in Spenser's sonnet cycle, *Amoretti*. As we saw in Chapter Seven, sonnets were originally, and predominantly, love lyrics from a male lover to and about a female beloved, and the sonnets in *Amoretti* are no exception. What does separate *Amoretti* from the herd is that Spenser utilizes them to court a very real and attainable woman—in this case, Elizabeth Boyle—and this courtship ends in marriage, which he records in the lovely poem, "Epithalamion."

In his sonnets, Spenser describes his deep love for Elizabeth while praising her various attributes, both physical beauties and spiritual virtues. In Sonnet 67, he almost gives up "after long pursuit and vaine assay," but to his surprise she turns to him "with her owne goodwill." Thus, in #68, he has something to celebrate, and he combines this celebration with that of Easter:

> Most glorious Lord of life! that, on this day,
> Didst make Thy triumph over death and sin;
> And, having harrow'd hell, didst bring away
> Captivity thence captive, us to win:
> This joyous day, dear Lord, with joy begin;
> And grant that we, for whom Thou didest die,
> Being with Thy dear blood clean wash'd from sin,
> May live for ever in felicity!
> And that thy love we weighing worthily,
> May likewise love thee for the same again;
> And for thy sake, that all like dear didst buy,
> With love may one another entertain!
> So let us love, dear Love, like as we ought:
> Love is the lesson which the Lord us taught.

The first four lines (known as a *quatrain*) establish "this day" as Easter in a number of ways. By referring to Christ as the

"Lord of life," Spenser echoes His own words to His disciples: "I am the way, the truth, and the life: no man cometh unto the Father, but by me" (John 14:6). Not only does Jesus *say* this, but He makes good His word on Easter morning when, as the angel at the empty tomb reports, "he is risen from the dead" (Matt. 28:7).

As the "glorious Lord of life," Christ "triumph[s] over death and sin," reminding us of Romans 6:23: "For the wages of sin is death; but the gift of God is eternal life through Jesus Christ our Lord." Spenser then refers to His having "harrow'd hell"; "According to medieval theology, even the most estimable of the Old Testament patriarchs had been subjected to spiritual privation until Christ made atonement for Adam's fall. Because they were eventually to be saved, however, those souls were permitted to dwell in the Limbo of the Fathers rather than in hell itself."[1] On Good Friday, when Christ descended into hell, He ended their "captivity," demonstrating His power to free "captive us," all those who are slaves to sin.

Spenser then returns to Easter itself, this "joyous day," and asks his Lord to "begin" it "with joy." Asking for "joy" on a "joyous day" may seem redundant, but it only serves to emphasize the speaker's elation. He then asks that those "for whom Thou didest dye / Being with Thy dear blood clean wash'd from sin, / May live for ever in felicity!" This request neatly joins the purpose of Christ's crucifixion—to wash away sin—and the purpose of His resurrection—to provide eternal life.

---

[1] David Bevington, "Medieval Drama," (Boston: Houghton Mifflin, 1975): 594.

Spenser can make this prayer in confidence, knowing that he is one of the "we" for whom Christ died and rose again.

As the prayer continues, he asks for two more gifts from Christ, gifts that correspond with the greatest commandments: "Jesus said unto him, Thou shalt love the Lord thy God with all thy heart, and with all thy soul, and with all thy mind. This is the first and great commandment. And the second is like unto it, Thou shalt love thy neighbour as thyself" (Matt. 22:37-39). In order to fulfill these commandments, Spenser acknowledges that it is through Christ's "love" that he "May likewise love [Him] for the same again." Furthermore, because Christ "didst buy" (that is, redeem from sin) "all" others, Spenser "With love may one another entertain." To "entertain" is to treat with hospitality, to open one's home to, to love one's neighbor as oneself. It is only because of Christ's supreme act of love that we are able to love Him and our neighbors as we should.

But lest we forget that the *Amoretti* sonnets are primarily romantic in nature, Spenser deftly turns from his prayer to God to address his beloved on the theme of love. Having established Christ's love for us, he tells her, "So let us love, dear Love, like as we ought, / Love is the lesson which the Lord us taught." Moving from loving one's neighbors in general, Spenser chooses a very particular neighbor, the one he wishes to marry. This may seem disingenuous at first, a sly ploy to convince Elizabeth that she "ought" to love him, but it is actually Spenser's way of modeling, as he does throughout *The Faerie Queene*, a virtue—the virtue of marital love. In effect, it is Spenser's version of Ephesians 5:21-33, especially St. Paul's directions: "Husbands, love your wives, even as Christ also loved the church, and gave himself for it; ... let every one of you in particular so love his wife even as himself; and the wife see that she reverence her husband." They are to love each other in response to Christ's love for them: Spenser will care for Elizabeth, his "dear Love," just as his "dear Lord" shed His "dear blood" for them. This is a worthy model for us all.

Questions for Contemplation

1. "Dear" means of great worth or great cost. Have you ever thought of your being "dear" to Jesus?

2. Imagine being a "captive," then imagine being set free. How would you respond to your savior?

3. What would it mean to you to love your spouse (or anyone close to you) for Jesus' sake?

Chapter Ten

————— • —————

PREPARATORY MEDITATION 2.26
BY EDWARD TAYLOR

E dward Taylor (1642-1729) had the benefit of inheriting the beautiful verse of Spenser, Bradstreet, Herbert, and Donne. Like Herbert and Donne, he was a minister; like Bradstreet, he was a Puritan, born in Great Britain, who came to the New World in search of religious freedom. And, like all of these predecessors, he found poetry to be an excellent way of meditating upon the word of God and of expressing his relationship with his Savior.

The majority of Taylor's poems are "Preparatory Meditations," poems reflecting on Scripture in preparation for a sermon he was going to preach. Meditation 26 (Second Series) is a response to Hebrews 9:13-14: "For if the blood of bulls and of goats, and the ashes of an heifer sprinkling the unclean, sanctifieth to the purifying of the flesh: How much more shall the blood of Christ, who through the eternal Spirit offered himself without spot to God, purge your conscience from dead works to serve the living God?" Taylor writes,

Unclean, Unclean: My Lord, Undone, all vile
    Yea all Defild: What shall thy Servant doe?
Unfit for thee: not fit for holy Soile,
    Nor for Communion of Saints below.

A bag of botches, Lump of Loathsomeness:
Defild by Touch, by Issue: Leproust flesh.

Thou wilt have all that enter do thy fold
    Pure, Cleane, and bright, Whiter than whitest Snow
Better refin'd than most refined Gold:
    I am not so; but fowle; What shall I doe?
    Shall thy Church Doors be shut, and shut out mee?
    Shall not Church fellowship my portion bee?

How can it be? Thy Churches do require
    Pure Holiness: I am all filth, alas!
Shall I defile them, tumbled thus in mire?
    Or they mee cleanse before I current pass?
    If thus they do, Where is the Niter bright
    And Sope they offer mee to wash me White?

The Brisk Red heifer's Ashes, when calcin'd,
    Mixt all in running Water, is too Weake
To wash away my Filth: The Dooves assign'd
    Burnt, and Sin Offerings neer do the feate
    But as they Emblemize the Fountain Spring
    Thy Blood, my Lord, set ope to wash off Sin.

Oh! richest Grace! Are thy Rich Veans then tapt
    To ope this Holy Fountain (boundless Sea)
For Sinners here to lavor off (all sapt
    With Sin) their Sins and Sinfulness away?
    In this bright Chrystall Crimson Fountain flows
    What washeth whiter, than the Swan or Rose.

Oh! wash mee, Lord, in this Choice Fountain, White
    That I may enter, and not sully here

Thy Church, whose floore is pav'de with Graces bright
  And hold Church fellowship with Saints most cleare.
My Voice all sweet, with their melodious layes
  Shall make sweet Musick blossom'd with thy praise.

Taylor begins by examining himself and by declaring, openly and honestly, just how much he is in need of his Lord: he is "Unclean, Unclean … Undone" and "Unfit," utterly unable to cleanse himself. His use of alliteration in describing himself as a "bag of botches, Lump of Loathsomeness … Leproust flesh" focuses the reader's attention on these sickly metaphors; "botches" are tumors while leprosy is the disease of supreme uncleanliness in the Bible (see, for example, Leviticus 13:11: "It is an old leprosy in the skin of his flesh, and the priest shall pronounce him unclean, and shall not shut him up: for he is unclean"). Such a condition renders Taylor "not fit for holy Soile, / Nor for Communion of Saints below;" in other words, he cannot come into God's presence nor can he serve the members of his own church. It is important to remember that he is not simply a member of his congregation but is the pastor himself; rather than seeing himself as somehow being superior to others, he openly confesses his sinful state.

This creates a dilemma for Taylor as he is the exact opposite of what God requires. He is "fowle" where God requires "Whiter than whitest Snow;" he is lumpish where God requires "Better refin'd than most refined Gold," echoing Zechariah 13:9 ("I … will refine them as silver is refined, and will try them as gold is tried"). This stanza ends with a series of despairing questions as Taylor envisions being "shut out" from "Church fellowship," barred from God's house, facing the same exile that a leper would have faced.

The questioning continues in the following stanza. Taylor wonders if God's "Churches" can clean him when he is "all filth" itself, not merely "tumbled … in mire." Mire implies mud and dung, an image that adds layers of filth to his leprous flesh. Given the extent to which Taylor embodies his unholiness, he cannot imagine the "Niter," a chemical cleansing agent, or the "Sope" that could "wash [him]White."

With no answers to his questions, Taylor turns back to Hebrews 9:13 and its list of Old Testament rituals of purification and the "Red heifer's Ashes." Furthermore, he adds, "The Dooves assign'd / Burnt, and sin offerings," thereby referencing Leviticus 5:7: "And if he be not able to bring a lamb, then he shall bring for his trespass, which he hath committed, two turtledoves, or two young pigeons, unto the LORD; one for a sin offering, and the other for a burnt offering." Note that Taylor is unable to provide a lamb but can bring only doves. Yet he recognizes that they are "too Weak / To wash away [his] Filth," incapable of rendering him white as snow.

But this stanza, unlike the previous three, does not end in a place of hopelessness, for even if the sacrifices of the Old Testament are not sufficient, they do "Emblemize the Fountain Spring / Thy Blood, my Lord, set ope[n] to wash off Sin." In other words, they prefigure "the blood of Christ, who through the eternal Spirit offered himself without spot to God" (Heb. 9:14). Here is the Lamb that Taylor could not sacrifice, "the Lamb of God, which taketh away the sin of the world" (John 1:29).

62

As soon as he mentions Christ's blood, Taylor exclaims with joy, "Oh! richest Grace!" This is the answer he has been seeking. Instead of asking questions from the position of the outcast, he now asks a rhetorical question to describe this rich grace that flows from Christ: it is a "boundless Sea," a limitless supply of grace expressly "For Sinners here to lavor [wash] off" not only "their Sins" but their inherent "Sinfulness" as well. By repeating "Sinners," "Sin," "Sins," and "Sinfulness" in a mere two lines, Taylor both layers on the filth and mire described earlier while also showing the power of God's grace to wash all of this away. It is the "bright Chrystall Crimson Fountain" of Christ's blood that washes the sinners so thoroughly—"Chrystall" is a favorite Renaissance pun on "Christ all" that connotes Jesus' purity,—and "Crimson" to remind us of the sacrificial blood.

Now that Taylor has realized the efficacy of Christ's blood for all sinners, he turns back to his own situation, exclaiming, "Oh! wash mee, Lord." It is through Christ's saving grace alone that he "may enter … Thy Church" and rejoin the "fellowship" of "Saints" that seemed to be so firmly separated from him in his filthy sinfulness. There, he will be able to join in their hymns, "their melodious layes," and "praise" God for all He has done. Where once Taylor had repeated words of "filth" and "Sin," he now repeats "sweet." The poem ends with—and contributes to—the "sweet Musick" of praise. We, too, participate in such washing and singing.

Questions for Contemplation

1. How do you try to wash away your own sinfulness? How do those efforts lead you away from Christ?

2. How might this poem relate to the waters of baptism?

3. Does this poem make you think about your fellow church members in a different way? How so?

Chapter Eleven

•————•————•

PREPARATORY MEDITATION 1.8
BY EDWARD TAYLOR

One of Edward Taylor's favorite subjects for his poetic meditations is Holy Communion. In many ways, he ponders how it is linked to Christ's words in John 6:51: "I am the living bread which came down from heaven: if any man eat of this bread, he shall live for ever: and the bread that I will give is my flesh, which I will give for the life of the world." What seems to be metaphorical here becomes firm reality at the Last Supper, when "Jesus took bread, and blessed, and brake it, and gave to them, and said, Take, eat: this is my body" (Mark 14:22). In Meditation 8 (First Series), Taylor contemplates the "Bread of Life" that he is graciously allowed to eat.

The poem's central organizing principle is how the Bread of Life makes its way from heaven to Taylor:

I kening through Astronomy Divine
    The Worlds bright Battlement, wherein I spy
A Golden Path my Pensill cannot line,
    From that bright Throne unto my Threshold ly.
    And while my puzzled thoughts about it pore
    I finde the Bread of Life in't at my doore.

When that this Bird of Paradise put in
      This Wicker Cage (my Corps) to tweedle praise
Had peckt the Fruite forbad: and so did fling
      Away its Food; and lost its golden days;
      It fell into Celestiall Famine sore:
      And never could attain a morsel more.

Alas! alas! Poore Bird, what wilt thou doe?
      The Creatures field no food for Souls e're gave.
And if thou knock at Angells dores they show
      An Empty Barrell: they no soul bread have.
      Alas! Poore Bird, the Worlds White Loafe is done,
      And cannot yield thee here the smallest Crumb.

In this sad state, Gods Tender Bowells run
      Out streams of Grace: And he to end all strife
The Purest Wheate in Heaven, his deare-dear Son
      Grinds, and kneads up into this Bread of Life.
      Which Bread of Life from Heaven down came and stands
      Disht on thy Table up by Angells Hands.

Did God mould up this Bread in Heaven, and bake,
      Which from his Table came, and to thine goeth?
Doth he bespeak thee thus, This Soule Bread take.
      Come Eate thy fill of this thy Gods White Loafe?
      Its Food too fine for Angells, yet come, take
      And Eate thy fill. Its Heavens Sugar Cake.

What Grace is this knead in this Loafe? This thing
      Souls are but petty things it to admire.
Yee Angells, help: This fill would to the brim
      Heav'ns whelm'd-down Chrystall meele Bowle, yea and higher.

> This Bread of Life dropt in thy mouth, doth Cry.
> Eate, Eate me, Soul, and thou shalt never dy.

Taylor begins by looking up at the night sky, imagining the "Divine" stars as the "bright Battlement," the top of the world's fortified walls, within which sits "that bright Throne" of God. He seems to see a "Golden Path" from it to his own home, a path by which "the Bread of Life" comes to his very "doore." This "puzzle[s]" him, because he cannot chart it but also, as will become more apparent in stanza three, cannot understand why it is so. His "Pensill" that cannot trace the path from God's throne room may be a pun on both *pencil*, a writing implement, and *pensive*, his thoughts on the matter. His "thoughts about it pore" or *pour*, but he is punning on *poor* to show the relative unworthiness of his dwelling compared to the "bright Throne."

The astronomical imagery of stanza one is replaced with new language in stanza two as Taylor puzzles over the appearance of the Bread of Life and his own need for food. He creates the comparison of his soul within his body to a bird in a cage: his soul is a "Bird of Paradise" because it comes from God. And like many a caged bird, his purpose is to sing, "to tweedle praise," *tweedle* serving as a way to disparage his own poetic attempts. But even in this he fails, for as did Adam and Eve before him, Taylor sinned, he "peckt the Fruit forbad[e]." Ironically, in choosing the forbidden fruit, he throws away his real "Food" and "fell into Celestiall Famine." His sinful fall separates him from the heavenly nourishment his soul requires, and he is unable to get it on his own for he "never could attain a morsell more."

His hopeless, helpless state is bemoaned in the next stanza, beginning with his cries of "Alas! alas!" Taylor considers, and then rejects, three possible sources of nourishment for his soul, the "Poore Bird." The first is "The Creatures field," presumably a field of grain where animals find sustenance and also where mortals grow wheat for bread, but such a field cannot provide "food for Souls." The second looks higher, to "Angells dores," but angels have nothing but "An Empty Barrell" as they have no need for food, "soul bread" or otherwise. Finally, Taylor notes that "the Worlds White Loaf is done." This may mean either that (a) the finest bread that the world can offer is worthless for his soul's needs, or (b) the sinlessness of man before the Fall is no longer available, not even "the smallest crumb."

In any case, Taylor's soul is left "in this sad state" at the very center of the poem. To continue thus means to starve to death. He can do nothing, but he is not forsaken, for "Gods Tender Bowells run / Out streams of Grace." The bowels are understood to be the seat of deep feelings in this time period, just as we place deep emotions in the heart. We read, for example, in Colossians 3:12: "Put on therefore, as the elect of God, holy and beloved, bowels of mercies, kindness, humbleness of mind ..." In Taylor's image, grace comes pouring out of God the Father, and He provides the only food that will feed Taylor's famished soul.

He envisions the incarnation of God the Son in very physical terms as God the Father "Grinds" "The Purest Wheate in Heaven," then "kneads up" "this Bread of Life." God the Son is molded into Jesus the man and served "up by Angells hands" as if angels are God's waiters. The "Table" is perhaps earth itself, but it is also the altar where Holy Communion is laid out.

Having imagined Christ's incarnation in this manner while recognizing the tremendous gift given to him—God's "deare-dear Son"—Taylor can hardly believe that it is true, that God would feed him in this way. In order to believe, the poet must hear God Himself, and so he presents God's invitation:

> This Soule Bread take.
> Come Eate thy fill of this thy Gods White Loafe?
> Its Food too fine for Angells, yet come, take
> And Eate thy fill. Its Heavens Sugar Cake.

Taylor is told to "take" the Bread and "Eate thy fill," echoing Christ's own command to "Take, eat: this is my body." Taylor adds "thy fill" to show His generosity. In fact, God repeats "Eate thy fill," making it abundantly clear that there is no limit to this feast. Christ's body is the "White Loafe … Heavens Sugar Cake," the finest food that can possibly be offered.

After such an invitation, Taylor seems overwhelmed: "What Grace is this knead in this Loafe?" It is limitless whereas the "Souls" that receive it are "but petty things" in comparison. Taylor tries to describe its vastness by picturing the dome of Heaven, inverted into a "Chrystall meele Bowle," as overflowing with such grace.

Miraculously, this grace, kneaded into the Bread of Life, is "dropt" into Taylor's mouth and speaks to him again: "Eate, Eate me, Soul, and thou shalt never dy." Even as the poet's soul seems incapable of answering God's command to "take" the Living Bread, God drops it into his mouth, through Holy Communion. Where once Taylor "never could attain a morsell more," now he shall "never dy" because God's grace, through His son, Jesus Christ, has come directly to him.

It is worth pointing out that Taylor's praise of God's grace continues in Meditation 9, where he demonstrates how the Bread of Life is far superior to the "Earthly Cookery" of all times and places. He ends this poem with a prayer: "feed mee all my days, / With Living Bread to thy Eternall Prayse." Thus, are we fed; To God be the Glory.

Questions for Contemplation

1. What does it mean to you that Jesus is the Bread of Life?

2. Does this poem give you a greater appreciation of Holy Communion? How so?

3. In what other ways does God manifest His grace toward you?

Chapter Twelve

"WHEN I CONSIDER HOW MY LIGHT IS SPENT" BY JOHN MILTON

No study of seventeenth-century Protestant poetry would be complete without an example of John Milton's works. Milton (1608-1674) is the most famous English writer of his time, having produced the last great epic poem before novels replaced poetry as the reading public's favorite genre. *Paradise Lost* retells the story of Adam and Eve, but it does so on a grand scale while exploring a number of theological and philosophical questions through the eyes of pre- and post-fallen humanity, Satan, the angels, and even of God Himself. It is a stunningly beautiful work of art, the Sistine Chapel of the literary world. And Milton was blind when he wrote it.

Of course, *Paradise Lost*, like its epic predecessor, *The Faerie Queene*, cannot be reproduced here, so we turn to a lyric work in a form that should be quite familiar now, the sonnet. Unlike Spenser, who used this form primarily for romance, or Donne, who used it primarily for prayer, Milton used sonnets for a wide variety of purposes, ranging from praising Henry Lawes, the famous song writer of the 1600s, to condemning a military attack on Protestants in Italy. There are also more personal subjects, including Sonnet 16, where he questions his value as a blind man:

When I consider how my light is spent

    Ere half my days in this dark world and wide,

    And that one talent which is death to hide

    Lodged with me useless, though my soul more bent

To serve therewith my Maker, and present

    My true account, lest He returning chide,

    "Doth God exact day-labor, light denied?"

    I fondly ask. But Patience to prevent

That murmur, soon replies, "God doth not need

    Either man's work or his own gifts. Who best

    Bear his mild yoke, they serve him best. His state

Is kingly; thousands at his bidding speed,

    And post o'er land and ocean without rest:

    They also serve who only stand and wait."

Milton begins with the problem of being blind at such a relatively young age. Given a proverbial 70 years to live (Dante takes his journey to the inferno at the half-way point of his life, which is 35), Milton is acutely aware that his "light is spent" while he has still "half" his "days" to go. Spent means gone or perhaps used up, as if Milton had been allotted a certain amount of light for his entire lifetime, but he has wasted it like the prodigal son. Now, without that light, he is in a "world" both "dark" and "wide," dangerous and unknowable.

Having spent his allowance of light, he is left with "one talent." This is an allusion to Matthew 25:14-30, particularly these verses: "Then he which had received the one talent came and said, Lord, I knew thee that thou art an hard man, reaping where thou hast not sown, and gathering where thou hast not strawed: And I was afraid, and went and hid thy talent in the earth: lo, there thou hast that is thine. His lord answered and said unto him, Thou wicked and slothful servant, thou knewest that I reap where I sowed not, and gather where I have not strawed: ... And cast ye the unprofitable servant into outer darkness: there shall be weeping and gnashing of teeth." Just as the servant in this parable is cast into darkness because he hid his talent, Milton acknowledges that it would be "death to hide" his one talent. His talent, of course, is writing poetry, a skill that is "Lodged" within him, put there by God, but it seems "useless" now that he is blind.

Although "death to hide" is a phrase inspired by the parable, it speaks also of Milton's pain. Like the athlete who suffers a debilitating injury and can no longer do what he loves, he fears a future where he can no longer produce poetry. Is there life for someone who cannot pursue his clearest goal, who cannot make use of his God-given talent?

Milton's need to answer this question is made all the more pressing by the fact that, despite his physical infirmity, his "soul [is] more bent / To serve" his "Maker": he is spiritually inclined towards serving God with his talent. Just as the servants in the Parable of the Talents must provide a "true account" to their master, Milton envisions a scenario in which God will "chide" or chastise him for his failure.

Yet, would that be fair, he wonders, given the circumstance that his "light" has been "denied," revoked; how can God demand "day-labor" when there is no daylight for Milton? But even as he asks this, he admits to the foolishness of the question, as the virtue of "Patience" puts a stop to any such muttering against God.

And it is here, as Patience "replies," that the sonnet takes a turn. Whereas the first eight lines of the sonnet present the problem of Milton's blindness in the context of the Parable of the Talents, the final six lines present the solution by offering a larger context, one which does not focus on his disability.

Patience reminds Milton that "God doth not need / Either man's works or his own gifts," so he should not concern himself with his inability to make use of his talent. The referent of "his" in "his own gifts" is purposefully ambiguous, so that the gifts are "man's" but are also, more significantly, God's gifts to man; in other words, God does not need His own gifts back.

If neither gifts nor works are required, is there anything Milton might do to serve his maker? After all, God is the King with "thousands" of angels, a heavenly host that follow His "bidding," who are restricted by neither geography nor fatigue—they "post o'er land and ocean without rest." What could Milton possibly offer?

The answer to this is nothing—he can give nothing to God. Yet he can still serve by *receiving* another gift from God: Milton can "Bear his mild yoke." This is a clear reference to Christ's words in Matthew 11:28-30: "Come unto me, all ye that labour and are heavy laden, and I will give you rest. Take my yoke upon you, and learn of me; for I am meek and lowly of heart: and ye shall find rest unto your souls. For my yoke is easy, and my burden is light." Milton's earlier question—does God demand "day-labor"?—is answered here as it is quite the opposite: rather than ask for labor, Christ relieves those who are burdened by labor.

It is Patience who reminds Milton of Christ's offer because patience may be required for those "who only stand and wait."

The virtue of patience appears 33 times in the King James translation of the New Testament, so it is impossible to know if Milton had any specific passage in mind. Still, these verses from St. Paul seem particularly apropos: "For we are saved by hope: but hope that is seen is not hope: for what a man seeth, why doth he yet hope for? But if we hope for that we see not, then do we with patience wait for it" (Rom. 8:24-25). These words may have consoled Milton as they are true for *all* believers; his physical blindness makes him no different from the rest of us who, through God's grace, have been offered Christ's light yoke.

Questions for Contemplation

1. Have you been frustrated in using your God-given talent in service to Him? How might Patience speak to that frustration?

2. Why is it important that we, like Milton, recognize that our own shortcomings or obstacles are not unique to us?

3. How might you use Milton's poem to minister to Christians who feel useless?

Chapter Thirteen

‑‑‑‑‑‑•‑‑‑‑‑•‑‑‑‑‑•‑‑‑‑‑

FINAL THOUGHTS,
FURTHER READINGS

C hildren love poetry.

Perhaps, now, that love has been re-awakened in you as you read, re-read, and contemplated these eleven examples of seventeenth-century Christian lyric poetry, composed by three preachers, two professional writers, and one housewife. All of them were quite prolific, and the Works Cited page at the close of this volume will provide you with the titles of their collections should you be inspired to read more.

As I have written elsewhere, as "a Lutheran English professor, I feel that it is of utmost importance to guide [my] students towards experiencing God's grace as it is expressed in literature."[1] But why should this experience be the domain of students only? In writing this book, I have, as it were, opened up the classroom doors and invited you in to meet some of my favorite authors.

Here, you have experienced the doubts and fears of Donne and Taylor, the griefs of Bradstreet and Milton, the gratitude of Spenser and Herbert. But more than that—oh, so much more—you

---

[1] "Mirror, Imagination, and Creation: A Lutheran Approach to Literature," in *The Idea and Practice of a Lutheran University*, ed. Scott A. Ashmon (Saint Louis, MO: CPH, 2015): 32.

How could God's people, both in the Bible and in the generations that follow, not praise Him in poems and songs?

have seen the unfailing grace and mercy poured out upon them by our savior, Jesus Christ, grace and mercy culminating in, as Bradstreet reminds us, "an house on high erect, / Framed by that mighty Architect, / With glory richly furnished."

With such a subject as this, how could God's people, both in the Bible and in the generations that follow, not praise Him in poems and songs? And, come to think of it, what's stopping you from joining the chorus?

WORKS CITED

Bevington, David. *Medieval Drama*. Boston: Houghton Mifflin. 1975.

Bunyan, John. *The Pilgrim's Progress*. Pocket Books, NY. 1957.

Divine Comedy of Dante, The. Henry Wadsworth Longfellow (trans.). USA: NuVision, 2007.

Donne, John. *The Complete English Poems*. London: Penguin Classics, 1971; rpt. 1987.

Gioia, Dana. "Christianity and Poetry." *First Things*, August 2022. https://www.firstthings.com/Article/2022/08/christianity-and-poetry

Herbert, George. *The Temple*. UK: Penguin Classics, 2017.

Milton: Minor Poems. Samuel Thurber, ed. Boston and Chicago: Allyn and Bacon, 1901.

Poems of Edward Taylor, The. Donald E. Stanford, ed. UNC, 1960; rpt. 1989.

Poetical Works of Edmund Spenser, The. NY: Crowell & Co.. n.d.

Tom, Kerri L. "Mirror, Imagination, and Creation: A Lutheran Approach to Literature," in *The Idea and Practice of a Lutheran University*, Scott A. Ashmon, ed. St. Louis: CPH, 2015.

Works of Anne Bradstreet, The. Jeannine Hensley, ed. Cambridge, MA: Belknap Press, 2010.